Bedroom Music

.

Bedroom Music

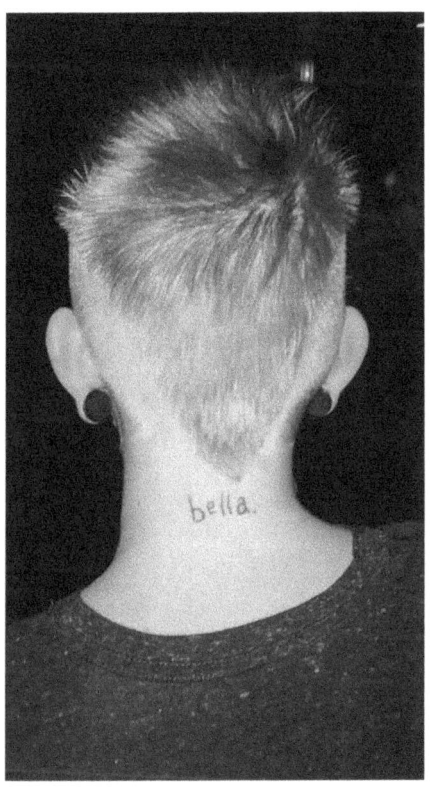

poems by
Steph Castor

STUBBORN
MULE
PRESS
DEVIL'S ELBOW, MO

Stubborn Mule Press
Devil's Elbow, MO
stubbornmulepress.com

First Edition 11 7 5 3 2 1
ISBN: 978-1-950380-00-8
LCCN: 2019933167
Design, edits and layout: Jeanette Powers
stubbornmulepress@gmail.com @stubbornmulepress
Cover Image: Elim J. Sidus
interior photo (and hair!): Valerie Castaneda
bio photo: Steph Castor

To pinwheel spinners and tequila dreamers; whiskey swimmers and calloused fingers...

Table of Contents

How to Give a Purple Otter Pop

1.

When you're riding your red Magna two-wheeler,
don't tighten your shoelaces.
Let the occasional tug
from your clumsy heels
ease the friction in your bunny knots.
Kick off with your right foot;
wobble the left
so you find your
balance.
Push hard.
Feel the burn in your calves
like your mom's
boyfriend's
sculpted deltoids.
Keep pushing— just long enough
to feel elated.
When you find your butterflies,
aim for the brush on the side of the road
and remember how it felt
when mom grabbed your seat
the first time
but couldn't catch you.
Fall with your hands first.
Look at your hands.
Pick the gravel from
the creases in your thumbs.
Don't pick your skin.
It doesn't need to hurt
worse than
it looks.
Go inside.
Don't fuss too much.
Just knock and pretend
that it still hurts.

2.

The moment you realize
you've started your first period.
You're anxious about it.
Wad up two feet
of toilet paper and
tuck it between
your legs.
You know there are tampons under the sink.
Turn on the television.
Keep the volume at 8.
Find *Rocket Power*,
but don't sing along this time.
You're too old
for that shit now,
and your mom is still
sleeping.
If you wake her,
she'll get all mom-like
and tell you about that time
in high school
when she smoked weed once
and met your dad
in a walk-in pantry
and how nice sex is
but you shouldn't have babies
until you've found a man
who deserves you.
You smirk at the thought.
Go outside
and avoid clichés
of your recent
fruitful womanhood.
Steal the keys.
Practice parking the car
in the driveway
and never leave.
Discover politics on AM radio.

You're too young
for that shit.
Realize that you are a poet
and compare the colors on the dashboard
to the rainbow assortment
in your freezer.
Go back inside
and write down what you saw.
Stay quiet. She is still sleeping.

3.

You're ashamed.
Your mom married
in Vegas
to the man you loathe.
You sneak a Grand Marnier
miniature
from their hotel room.
You cannot stay
in their hotel room.
You're forced to stay
with your grandmother
who passes gas
when she steps on the brake pedal
too hard.
You open up to her
about your dream
of one day playing
the guitar.
You listen to The Smiths too much
and write fake proposals
to Johnny Marr.
She says the guitar
is a feminine instrument
and that
Papa played a hummingbird.
You suddenly don't mind the gas

and show her how you like to
ease the brakes.
You think you're drunk,
but you're just thirsty,
so you ask to go
to a gas station.
You buy her a popsicle
with leftover Easter money,
even though you don't
celebrate it.
Suddenly,
you notice
how the Vegas strip
matches the dashboard.

4.

You think you've found a man
who deserves you,
so you pierce your ears.
You spend your spare change
on making out with him
and his stale gum
at the Edwards Cinema.
You start thinking about
strawberries
and how they are always the brightest
in Santa Maria.
Perhaps the sweetest
but you would never know.
You hate strawberries.
You realize you are still making out
with that boy
and he didn't even buy popcorn.
You go to the bathroom
and call your mom
to tell her about the man
who might deserve you

but never buys popcorn.
She says he's no man
and that you should get home
right now.
You take the bus home
and find her on the couch.
You sit and
she puts her arms
around you.
She tells you she's proud,
you're important,
her world.
Her eyes are puffy
neck— purple.
You look around and see
empty corners.
You get up and walk to the kitchen.
You pour her a glass
of ice water
and reach into the freezer.
You pull out two purple
Otter Pops
because they are
your favorite.
You hand one to her.
You teach her how to fall
with her hands first
and how you discovered
poetry
in the driveway
and how you got drunk
with Grammie in Las Vegas.
She smiles.
Squeezes your hand.
And you fall asleep.

Rip; Curl

I'm innocent.
I swear.
Not really.
I've betrayed the sea
and bought friends with faux shells.
The sand
under my nails
is unbearable,
so I give the dollars
to Charity:
a four-year-old
beach blondie
sitting next to her
plastic red pail
and eroding castle.
I envision myself
in the moat,
fleeing the sharks
and hoarding current.

The spindrift spits on my face,
harsh but sugared.

Recess

I can think of my most basic being
as the 5th grade spelling bee runner up.
I spit on the gravel plane where my knuckles
invented their scars.

That handball zephyr war
where we played with words
as if they could keep tallies
of our empty swings.

Hacienda Avenue

My morning cartoon and toaster ritual where I kissed my first boy.
The swing set runway where I wanted to throw up
because I kissed my first boy.
The lunchtime catastrophe on the soccer field
behind an oak tree
where I kissed a Catholic girl
because we wanted to know what sex felt like.

Astronaut

Not from Apollo 13; not Tom Hanks
and sure as hell not
Ron Howard's green screen bitch.
Not a victim of re-entry in 2003.
Not a Star Trek zealot
though Spocko and McCoy knew
how to handle those heaters.
Not an orange jumpsuit naval coach,
the phony kind of star skater
with hickies from black holes;
the cosmically fucked kinetic kitsch
tripping over stitching in
the sidewalk.
The quasi-apple bottom vegan
with the static sun
as an excuse not to run.
Not even in place.
Not even for Lymphoma Awareness.
Not even in the sand
on North Beach
on a sex driven stroll
with a woman they call "Wizard."
Not even dark matter maritime.

A Structured Exegesis

I come from foreign liberation and weird
holes in my ears with all shades of pride and moderate
temper as I have bathed with the dolphins and never feared
my own death outside of volatile wind and confederate
shotguns to the six worry lines on my forehead, never cured
of the cocaine coffee table at age nine, defined
as powdered sugar that I refused to blanket on that day's obscured
dessert. It was so pure, white, sweet, and refined,
and I can't help but remember the alimony
and what we left behind, for Mother had to scoot
our home into a garage and store knives next to My Little Pony.
We drove through cacti and snow without pause in commute
to Kansas, then Chicago, then back to Kansas for "love"
is more than just a Mother, but a filthy latex glove.

Chicago Pretty

I am a Midwest anachronism caught in a manhole,
happy like a drunk nun being felt up by a woman in
a business suit.

Sometimes, I want to snuggle with homeless men in Grant Park
     and ask them
to tell me recess stories from their childhood.
Chicago pretty—the industrialized kind of beautiful.
Like Coke bottles.

The simple display of drowning.

"I will live forever! Or die trying..."

No one wins.
I must quench my cheeks.

"Maybe if we drink each other's spit we'll get more drunk."

The simple display of drowning
     or the fact that coffee tastes like muddy shit.
          Coffee puts moths in my belly.
I need more. I need to be
happy like a drunk nun, dancing and sniffing blue pixie sticks.

We said dance.
Ferment the finite light.
Release it, then manipulate and explore a perfect woman.
She has money from elaborate beauty.
She was hit by a car today.
No parking except Sundays and Holidays.
        Happy like a drunk nun who plays without frowning.

She was too swift for them.

    "Your face looks like a swollen menstrual cycle."

"You can see me after class."

Yes. For coffee. Coffee tastes like muddy shit
and puts moths in my belly. Sometimes ugly ones.
It keeps me awake.
I don't feel comfortable on my bunk bed.
Allen Ginsberg is collecting dust below me.
So is the French poet with
an obscure name I can't pronounce.

Sometimes, I want to snuggle with nuns
with faces like swollen menstrual cycles.
Happy and drunk.

"Mamas can be the biggest heroes."

I don't feel safe in my bed.
Expose the night.
          Ferment the finite light.
Don't get hit by cars, and be home for dinner at seven.

"Maybe if we drink each other's spit we'll get more drunk."

The simple display of drowning.
Chicago pretty.

Lovelier Bones

She had driven through nothing
contending under the strain of the day by day
relieved to see the waves,
"The Awakening"
and Virginia Woolf.
—filmy stones down the cliffs
after tying down her feet.
Mother's desire to reach
the other side of thinking...

"You can start over again."
         Running from enclosed sandy boots
         with a stuffed white lamb wearing black
         she remembered she had the day around making sure
         —sure that someone held her hair back
         and there was distant screaming; a few guns.
         Disappointment overtook her arms
         and started singing.
         The rest, forgotten.
         Days long past, together on her plate.
"Hey, Ocean Eyes... where'd you go on us?"

Wizard Wishes

"You are impossible.
I could give you maniacal sex
and homemade peanut butter cups.
You won't let yourself love,
and I am adequate at least.
Here, on this concrete bridge.

Do it.

I won't tell anyone
if you want to indulge in me.
I know your body.
No one else knows your body
for its constellations.
They'd rather play
dot-to-dot on your shoulders.
I am not asking for forever yet.
I'm asking for the opportunity.

Yesterday, on the train,
you bit my lip.

Tonight we are fighting in Grant Park.
My roommate is in love with me again.
You are selfish and envious.
You are everything I want.
You are the frozen waves at Ohio St. Beach—
polluted and brittle.
You are the syncopation in a jazz song—
forced and stunning.
You are the heart of an artichoke—
tender with slivers.

Why won't you love me?
Why won't you love me?

Our imperfections
are not coincidental.
They are jigsawed,
the way our ears hook
when we press our breasts together.
Like what we are doing now.

I am ductile,
the way I am spun around you."

Wilburn

He spoke eucalyptus.
Released Cherry Swisher syllables.
And footnotes
to panning for gold
and prospecting
in sumptuous
California
mountain
ranges.

Mute Project

catch them
count them
collect the spiders
they creep up the arms
of infants
born from existential
mothers
they are not clean
they are not clean
they are precious frauds
silent
save me
ring around the rosie
babies born as coke fiends
ashes ashes
chemical lullaby

Lift Hill

I pictured the wooden troughs in her retinas
to be at a lesser elevation.
When we came to our dry tongues twisting
at the last crank, the last jolt,
I swallowed and threw out my blemished lips
toward the sorbet threads
above her whipping hair.

Her nerve-damaged fingers. My prosthetic callouses,
matching each other in syncopated waves,
like fucking.
Like owning each other
and the magazines
our hands stuck to.

Bonnie

I wrote a song for my best friend
and drew a white rose for her father.
We sat on dunes together,
and she drank her wine at fourteen.

If I could keep her closer
I'd find more to say.
Seven years back,
I'd have finished the stem, the thorns, and the shading.

Six months from now,
she'll drink her wine on the beach,
and what more will I have to say than:

"Congratulations. Sorry I couldn't be all I needed to be.

Come see me sometime."

Roamer

If you stare at a star long enough,
they all start to fall.
Drowsy begins.
Sober trip to God and
four unbiased, unbound preachers—
conveyors to virgin ears.
Tremble.
Tremble.
Damned tongues go to waste,
lacking catch phrases.
As a goddess, it's easy to pretend to fly.
Put on your play clothes
and go outside so the birds can cascade
to your make believe routine.
You are not heaven, exactly.
You blow kisses.
The wind, chafing.
Inhale me and the inviting glass, spilling
"The stars are not what they seem to be.
I know nothing."
We are bound to find another
with intention to taste.
Amorous, slicing through the cotton crush,
you contact—penetrate.
Sometimes we just want to pour in shame.
The shade is a mismatch
and it's raining sex again.
For some of us, the sound of it
is too much.
There's a flood outside.
The gutters are calling your name.
You're pruned and ghostly—
coat like a body bag.
You hear a stranger's voice
on your mother's machine.

He's the man in the movies
and she trusts that you
appreciate him
like she does.
He finds you sound asleep,
dreaming of worms,
and sweating.
Leaves drift across
the driveway.
Dew spits on your mother's brow—
pissing on her blouse.
The wind is so persuasive.
We've all betrayed the sea.
You, for the stars.
Me, for the same, delayed in mid-chase.
Falling fast,
swallowing gravel
with naked knees.

From the Anglican Priest Who Swears Like a Sailor

"We live our lives assuming things will happen.
We are the only animal with an extended childhood.
We have lost our body hair.
It's something that follows.

Let's harvest the body.
The liver is the only organ capable of complete regeneration.
(Put a .45 behind his ear, pull the trigger, and send his family
the bill for the casing)

Disconnect the kids from the Life Support System.
Medical tourism:
One fetus is better than three.
Zero is better than one.

They are willing to sell their kidneys to Westerners with money.

Prior to the sixties, they killed babies
by keeping them in the corner of the hospital.
This is mostly for your edification.
If you don't really understand microbiology, skip this chapter.

Sexual selection has pushed us to where we are now.

What is the difference between herpes and love?
Herpes last forever."
He had a vasectomy. He reminds me of my grandfather.
He is totally accessible and absolutely hates George W. Bush.

We live our lives assuming things will happen.
Light as well as time appears in packets.
Eighty-five percent of the universe shouldn't be there.
Dark matter.

No one holds a candle to a chimpanzee.

Seven Miles to Callender Road

Her shoelaces tango
with the weeds and burrs.
I wonder if she knows
her socks are dirty.
The Nyquil dissolves
my insides.
I hallucinate.
Maybe
the Sun is swallowing me.
I want to
tell Mom a fever is
eating me.
She pushes me
down the road
in a shopping cart.
We stumble
and the wheels spin
like a drunk horse
in heels.
We bury ourselves.
She heaves forward.
Molten lava,
orange like
the Mesa's face.
I can see the Mesa from here.
Mom tries to save me
but her socks
are still dirty.
Why
aren't they burning?
I want
to ask her
why she is crying
but we'll be home
soon.

9th and Emery

Her toenails sharpen by the hour. She blames the cat, but I blame the musty grease in the crevices of her nails for making it sting more. At least her skin is buttery. It's interesting how she lingers like nuts. Cashews, to be specific. Her breath creams on me. It resonates all crunchy. We sit, and it gets silent. It's silent because my eyes are closed and trying to acknowledge her sweet breath. They let the rest of my body indulge for a while. But she doesn't feel that when she strokes my fingertips. She feels calluses and loss. She feels me like a hollow shell with the ocean inside. I taste like brown sugar when I lie. My breath sounds icy and brief and like I'm trying to swallow dry bread. What do we do from here? We let go of each other's calluses. We run our fingers through the cat's downy littered coat. We open our eyes.

Industrial Affair

I am not the lakeshore sneeze blessed by
acid rain and trains derailing
outside classroom windows on Mondays.
The fog knows my real name and fails to
extinguish the rough fingertips that
graze the lips of his mistress who calls
me her knight and sleeps, deprived of
moonlight and is so formally dressed
in Greek brown in Greek Town, just west
of my head-to-toe mirror of smug
reflection blanketed in smog
and dog parks with sometimes vacant benches.
A man robbed me of my tide, so I took his dog
and gave it to my lady before she flew into the tracks.

Easier, Healthier, Happier

When you work in customer service,
it's important
not to let people know that you're grieving.
Most companies
make it their policy.
It's in your job description
to ply your lips
in an upturned angle
and grin
for the sake of the next
sticky-mouthed
aspartame junkie
feeling welcomed—
they pay your bills.

You begin to notice
the strands of saliva
that stretch across a woman's teeth
when they glaze over a menu.
You take note of the grooves in her gums
and understand that she doesn't floss.
Neither do you.
You begin some internal rants
about how 20 dollars
should buy a week's worth
of vegetables and black beans.
You look at her,
and she reminds you
of your mother-in-law.
Your mother-in-law is diabetic.
Your mother-in-law died this morning.
You smile
and nod
and be patient
and satisfy the customer.

The woman orders
a Mountain Dew
for her nine-year-old daughter.
She feeds her flame retardant.
For a minute, you see yourself
in that little girl,
and you hate her.
Her ratted sun-soaked hair,
the spaces between her teeth,
her long, tan, and
unshaven legs
complete with
her long, tan, and
furry arms
shoved in the pockets
of her silver gym shorts
matched with ankle socks
and black Nike basketball shoes.
She shovels candy into her mouth.
It starts to rain.
You wonder where her coat is,
and you hate her mother for that.
You see her fillings
between the red syrup and
plasticky masticated mulch
of Twizzlers.

You've never had a cavity.
Your wisdom teeth are coming in.
You don't have health insurance.
You are worried
you will get sick
if you don't have health insurance
and you will die
before you realize
what your ailment is.

So you commit to stop eating candy.

First Time

I fucked you three times
before I saw you naked.
I wouldn't let you touch me.

Maybe it's because
a monster haunts me.

Maybe it's because
I'm terrified to think
your mouth is beautiful,
even though I already
know it is.

You are a ritual
masterpiece
chiming near my
clip-on bow tie,
teaching me
somehow
not to die
with your zodiac
self-destruction.

Home Is Where Our Legs Are

When I look east
I see a storm with platinum hair
and thin toes painted childhood
like my pink shag carpet
at three years old.

I smell Thursdays in August,
cleaning Dad's kitchen and
sneaking a taste
of his roommate's
Italian brandy
from the top of the fridge.

When I look east
I look invincible
with my hand in
her back pocket.
She tightens her piano thumbs
around my ribcage.
My lungs begin to warm,
washing out
the second-hand black,
and hold strong to her
shot-gunned smiles.

When I look east
I see grass that is
brick, indigo,
salmon, teal, mauve,
lavender like her skin
in the morning
while I'm tonguing
my coffee and watching her sleep.
I see grass that's
anything but green.
I look for confetti and

parade eggs smashed
over our heads.

When I look east
I am organic
and sedimentary
like the remains
of rainy day sand dollars
I collected at
five years old.
I tried to use them
sparingly.

When I look east
I see her legs stretch like
wooden planks
where I am meeting my fate
at the edge.

When I look east
I see October evenings
and wine-stained teeth
while we are thumbing through
our next destination.

St. Louis

You were anxious
about leaving your
dogs behind.
The van froze,
as it always does
when Andrew drives.
But the green sky
smothered us,
and you were afraid
to lay
in the bunk
alone,
so you called
for me
to keep
you safe.

I coiled around you
like a static puppy,
hoping it
would make you
miss them less.
Our breaths
grated like
rumble strips
while the wind
tossed us
like a bag of
salt water taffy
until we learned
to stick to the
new car scent
and plastic
under our feet.

Cyanotypes

Blue
is not the color
of the ocean
you slept by
and blew kisses to
on the 101
in passing

—not the patterns
of dripping popsicles
between your toes
or dusty concrete
front porch steps—

not the ruffled
twin sheets;
hosts to your
freeway fucking.

Blue
is knuckles against
plaster
—are your
pharmaceutical friends—
is her hair
threading through
your sweater
on the home stretch.

Blue
is her
tracing the cracks
in your upturned lips,
fighting hard against
salty Chicago
tunnels

—is her
letting you write
sloppy, quick hand
rhymes
with cartoon ballads
in the background—
projecting.

A Brief Shower Scene

It would be too easy to leave
marks on things that
shouldn't be seen.
I'd have put my fist
through glass
if you weren't
drunkenly
singing.

Crosspen

I stabbed myself with a rocket
to see if I would combust.

I wish you'd smile when I write,
and I wish I could walk with you
to help you sweep
the messes others make.

Especially my own.

I wish I wasn't so messy for you.
I wish I was all backbone.

Vermont

we were in the backseat
drunken smiles and dirty feet
dancing on the passenger side
you tugged my hand past
a love lush mountain man
and pressed into me like that

dirty old backseat

New Hampshire

Your bruises are
blueberry pies.
I want to taste them
every time you sing.

I want to nibble your ears
like
vanilla taffy.

I want to feel you stretch
under my tongue
and twist
into mysterious flavors.

Massachusetts

Melody makes me want her harder—
like she might disappear at the end of this bar

or fall off every sharp.

Paraphernalia

I tried to write your name in the sand,
but you stopped me at the "S"—
said you hated your name;
that you didn't exist.

Then lightning struck,
turning your curves into glass.

You have shells under your skin
that tarnish my nails
when I pull you closer
and you pull apart.

Little do you know
that breathing is an art,
and you inhale
with such luxury
every time
you take a hit—
as if breathing
never needed
practice.

Cliché Sad Song

So I'm an asshole
and I'll bet you know it
but I never stopped digging
my nails into your skin
every time we kiss.

And I'm an asshole
for loving the taste of your spit
when you're drinking.

And I'm an asshole
who might write you a slow song
but I'll bet you'd find me sinking
into a melody I'd rather hear you sing.

And I'm an asshole
who looks at old photos of you
smiling and maybe wasted
off whiskey
and tasting my eyelids at 3 am.

And I'm an asshole
who "doesn't deserve you"
or the words you bend around my neck.

And I'm an asshole
who can't pick a movie
or pick up a bar tab
or choose what to eat,
who steps on your toes
when you try to dance with me,
who picks fights and throws things
out of jealousy,
who can't stand not to be seen
by you.

But I'm the asshole
who brings you coffee,
creates a shield when you sleep,
pictures you in music magazines,
and loves the way your hair does itself
in the morning.
Who also loves the taste of your spit when you wake.
Who traces the hurricane on your nude leg.
Who plans mystery candlelit dates
in bedrooms
on floors
in trailers
on the beach—
and falls apart, comes undone at the seams
when nothing works out perfectly.

But I'm the asshole
who will never get you
no matter how much
my liver can take.

And I'm the asshole
who can't stop trying
to tell you what it means
to be your whiskey
and lilies
and everything in between.

Who won't stop sobbing
and making everything about me,
afraid you'll never feel anything.

I'm the asshole
who just keeps saying
"I'm sorry."

Yellow Lush

If you get dizzy
I'll put flowers in your hair
and kiss you hard on the temple
'til I taste nectar.

And when your mother's baby
learns your name
I'll make sure she says it pretty
like blackout colors
on your ceiling.

We've gone too far to say
we're ashamed of the hues
we haven't seen.

Your smile feels like violet
when I come home.

The Verdict

You killed a bottle of vodka.
I sipped shit Pinot from a box...

... but not before wisecracking and smashing a few cans:
sweating cylinders of "America."

Neither of us knew how to focus
on each other.

Yet when the temperature bowed out,
we never loved harder,

huddling together,
rocking, on the concrete.

Kansas City always looks dead
in the dark—

the silence
in the bar across the street

the lack of echoes
in the presumed gunfire

the skyscrapers slowly dimming
their patriotic flickers to a sunken orange.

Night Watch

You're breathing faster in your sleep.
I'm counting nightmares.

I hope you forget.
I hope you forget.
I hope you forget.

Lottery

I'll never be a wife with a door prize
or a sack of gold
to cure the itch in your throat.

Honey/Whiskey

I spend my words in a parked car
and stay buckled in
—engine off like your hat is tipped
and it's your curly hair that gets me.
The way it sticks in the sink to
your gin spit
and nail-clippings.
I know how you want to hate me.

I really wish you would
so we'd be spared the
single bed and
distant wooden planks.
I love her more than I loved you.

I fuck her more
than I ever fucked you.
And she comes
all over my words
like they were always meant
for her.

I've been a wayward bat
blind as your peripherals in
our living room on
Tuesday nights.
You insisted on gin.
I stuck with whiskey,
because I wanted a girl
who would go down
like whiskey
—and she does.

That slow flame
viscosity
like molten honey

flirting down my chest.

She knows how to spell
"infinite"
with her tongue out.
I welcome it with backbeats
on her hipbones.
You've never known a me
like me
when she's singing beneath
my earlobes.
You've never known a me
like me
when ice plant and sand dunes
take hold.

It's your curly hair that gets me,
and hers
is yellow lustrous
gold rush
city streets.

Now please,
wipe the fucking sink.

Yard Games

I smell burning beer cans
and your bright yellow jacket
tightening
over bon fires.
We only pretend
we know
the rules.

9th and Burnside

I want to drink
your cream kiss and
lipstick
savor your tender
amaretto
your daffodil collar.

I want to etch
your body into the
Burnside brick
and draw
chalk hearts
with imperfect
curves.

Buzzard Beach

What if I wasn't meant
to be your escape plan?
Maybe I'm just a pile of mulch,
at your dog's paws,
staring upward
and hoping
to get lodged
in your soles.

What if I wasn't
a wretched prude,
waiting on the bar patio
at the burst of an overweight raindrop
colliding against my skull?

What if I was
still a happy drunk,
falling over
your honey that
has turned to
lavender,
yet newly minted
and silver
according to my
confused and desperate
touch?

Sunny Day

It is with slight embarrassment
that I keep peering
over my shoulder
at the mineral deposits
on the fire escape
hoping the door slams
through the muted
cushions of
my headphones,
hoping your platinum skull
peers through the
opening and
turns from silhouette
to a glowing greet.
I want to see the
flicker from your
pink lighter
flash against the
picnic table
I've crossed my legs at
and vandalized my
Bic ink signature into.
It has only been
sixty minutes
and something like
fifty feet,
but I want you
to wish
I was home.

Shift

Where have your softer sides gone?
Your curses, screaming,
running for the door—
footprints in the dirt
like you're heading somewhere sacred
so we won't find you anymore.

Tell me how to do it.
Tell me how to use you—
think I might lose it.
"Come and get me."

The howling dog won't scratch her itch
when she knows you're watching—
clawing at your legs
like you're trying to shake it all off—
think the ground is breaking
from too many spoiled houses.

Tell me how to do it.
Tell me how to lose you—
think I might lose it
again and again and again.

La Jolla

I wanted to feel safe
so I placed your photo
in every room, I slept.

I can't spell your name
in the moss
when I want to.

I mistake mussels
for guitar picks,
surprise myself;

like what I want
to say is just
under my cuticles.

This isn't the first time here.
It was warmer in the winter.

October 10th

boots crossed
ankles laced
coffee paints
foggy head, cozy face

nonsensical
remember to be, make sense, foggy feet
when water pounds
coffee drops

twisted head
cocaine chase
backwards tongue
taste time
amphetamine pace
how many weeks
drinking dizzy

your hair
smells like
warm drum beats
city scenes

mouth feels
like cake
hot tea
the Pearl District
burns perfectly

Cravings

Give me warm green grass
iced coffee
and stuttered first date lists.

Give me sticky tables
double whiskeys
and third date stories.
Give me cold air
green beer
and day five body glory.
Give me chai tea
Disney movies
and bookstore discoveries
while I ruminate
your neck.

Bartender's Logic

Whiskey is whiskey
and gin is gin
when it all keeps us
warm in our stomachs.

Twenty-four isn't so scary when you're
fucking a storm.

Twenty-five isn't so scary when you're
fucking a storm.

Twenty-six is a little frightening.

Twenty-seven

Twenty-eight

Twenty-nine is fucking terrifying, but I'm alive.

So let's have another Jamo
and call it good.

Steph Castor has slept in many beds, mostly because she started playing music over 18 years ago. From Walmart parking lots, to damp gas station grass in Montana, to van bench seats, to her cozy Eudora farm— let's just say each place she's laid her head comes with its own shit. Its own fire. Its own story. When she's not powering, enjoying living room band practice, or getting a bangover on stage with her band, Vigil and Thieves, Steph Castor acts as a freelance content writer, merchandiser, marketer, photographer, doodler, baker, and all around adventurer. Past work can be found in notable music outlets including Guitar Girl Magazine, Guitar World, Revolver Magazine, Tattoo.com, Outburn Magazine and many more. She is very happy to being joining the Stubborn Mule Press family.

@stephcastor
stephcastor.com
vigilandthieves.com

CPSIA information can be obtained
at www.ICGtesting.com
Printed in the USA
BVHW031745060319
541951BV00001B/109/P